Where Your Letter Goes

by
Kristin Cashore

Scott Foresman
is an imprint of

PEARSON

Glenview, Illinois • Boston, Massachusetts • Mesa, Arizona
Shoreview, Minnesota • Upper Saddle River, New Jersey

I will show you how the mail works.
First, I write a letter to my aunt in a faraway town. I write about school. I draw a picture of me, my parents, and my dog.

I put the letter in an envelope and seal it. I write my aunt's address on the envelope in my best handwriting.

Then I put a stamp on the envelope.
I make sure it sticks. I don't want it to
wash away.

I go to the mailbox near my home.
My dog keeps me company. I open the
box and drop the letter in.

A mail carrier empties the mailbox. He brings the mail to a post office. It is sorted and put on a truck. Then it goes to all parts of the country.

Mail carriers deliver the letters, even
if it's raining or cold. The mail carriers
put the letters in the right mailboxes.
   At last, my aunt gets my letter! She is
so happy. I hope I get an answer soon!